SuperQuick™ Solutions

Web Essentials

Time & Money Saving Tips for
Website, Social Media & e-Commerce

**Easy Pointers to Quickly Implementing and Managing
Website and Social Media Marketing Strategies**

These Solutions are Super Fast & Super Cost-Effective (& mostly FREE)!

Find Answers here for Websites, Smart Phones and e-Commerce!

This Book will show you how to harness the power of Digital Marketing, step-by-step, with great FREE sources and time saving tips!

Learn the Mysteries of
Free Shopping Carts, Free SEO, Social Media, and where to find Great FREE tools on the web

**If you were trying to figure out how to *cost-effectively* get
<u>fully integrated</u> Website, Smart Phone and Social Media Solutions
—with e-Commerce, Surveys and blogs —
here is your Answer - Revealed!**

By M. Nicole van Dam

Nicole is not an employee of Adobe, Apple, Amazon, Wordpress, Facebook or of any developer or social media business, and Nicole is not paid by any of them for the recommendations she makes in this book. Her only affiliation with these companies is that she uses them to address her digital media marketing solutions for her own creative and teaching endeavors. Because Nicole had to teach herself how to cost-effectively find digital marketing solutions, she wanted to make it easier for others to follow her footsteps. All of Nicole's recommendations in this book are based on her own experience and learning, and Nicole has not been paid for any of the recommendations that she makes in this book. In other words, Nicole's recommendations are based on the fact that these steps have worked for her, and she hopes that your experience is the same.

NO WARRANTY, WHETHER EXPRESS OR IMPLIED: Because Nicole is not a developer of any of the websites, services and software recommended in this book (collectively, the "Digital Solution Materials"), Nicole cannot warrant how well any of the Digital Solution Materials will work for you. Nicole wrote this book solely to describe how she, as a busy entrepreneur and entrepreneurship instructor, has used these Digital Solution Materials to create her strategic digital presence, and that she believes that these Digital Solution Materials have been a cost-effective answer for her website, smart phone and marketing needs. Nicole cannot and does not offer a warranty of any kind, whether express or implied, in connection with the Digital Solution Materials or your use of this book or any of the Digital Solution Materials. In addition, the Digital Solution Materials are quite likely to change over time, over which changes Nicole has no control or input. Without limiting the generality of the foregoing, Nicole is not warranting that any of the Digital Solution Materials are suitable for any particular use or purpose; Nicole is merely showing in this book how she herself has used the Digital Solution Materials.

To contact the Publisher: SuperQuick Publications, P.O. Box 583, Ojai, CA 93024
Website: SuperQuick.bz
Email: SuperQuickBooks@aol.com

About the Cover Art*: "Sailing™" is a painting by M. Nicole van Dam.*

How to Get a Business Website on the Web that works with Smart Phones too!

The way to use this book is to have it open on your lap while you work on your computer – this book is a step-by-step illustrated guide to great resources on the web that will make it much easier to create an effective internet presence and implement and manage social media and other online marketing strategies.

Implementing the material in this book allows you to control your web-destiny, your smart-phone destiny, your social media and e-commerce destiny, and shows you how to make more money from affiliations with Google, Amazon and YouTube, that they pay YOU for. The best part about this book is that much of what you need to create an engaging and lucrative internet presence is here, all **without paying someone by the hour to develop your internet strategy**. In other words, the powerful (and many FREE) tools in this book will make this an indispensable reference, and we believe you will find your visible results worth the effort.

To see More Helpful Books from SuperQuick™ Solutions, please visit SuperQuick.bz

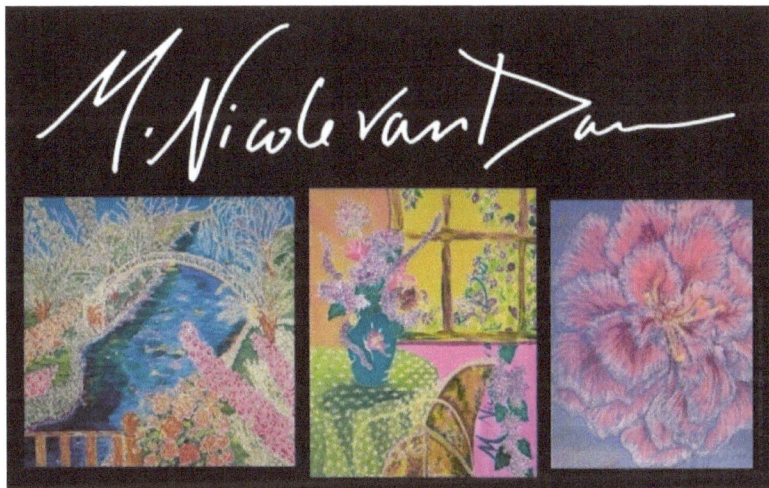

To see the artwork of the author and explore the author's own web presence, please visit Nicole.bz

**The Solution to your Business Website and
Smart Phone Needs –
That is why this effort is worth doing.**

Table of Contents

Prelude

We hope that this Book is of great use to You!

M. Nicole van Dam has been forging her own unique niche in the art world, and to do this she has had to conquer website design in a cost-effective way. Nicole wrote this book so that it would be easier for others to spend time on their Creative endeavors/field of choice, rather than on trying to demystify how to get a presence on the web.

To see the artwork of the author on her own Wordpress site,
please visit Nicole.bz .

Part 1 - Getting Started

Section 1: What common things might a
business owner/entrepreneur/artist wish to accomplish online?

- Build your Brand

- Educate the world about your business

- Look professional

- Provide convenient, reliable access – have your business known as a consistent,

reliable presence online and accessible via mobile

- Build community/customer loyalty

- Keep in touch with clients

- Market your products/services to existing clients

- Market your products to entirely new clients

- Provide user-friendly product/service education

- Provide effective Product/service support

- Learn more about your target Demographic

- Do Product Research

- Sell your products/services on the web:

    - Locally

    - Nationally (watch state laws – different states might have different laws)

    - Internationally (watch export/import laws!)

Section 2: Might there be some negatives to consider?

The negatives you should consider in devising your web strategy fall into three main categories:

- Technology Negatives – digital world keeps changing, so many inconsistent platforms (example iphone Flash issue; competing mobile platforms, creating a publication in the format for iBook not the same as the format for Nook and also not the same as the format for Kindle, etc.)

- Strategic negatives (such as revealing your customer lists and future plans (more detail on this below))

- Intellectual Property negatives (such as compromising the enforceability, control and even ownership of your intellectual property (more detail on this in Section 3))

What You Don't Want to Accomplish

- Giving away your customer list

- Revealing your future plans before you're ready

- Posting things that seem OK now but embarrass later

- Giving away what you really should be selling

- Compromising your Intellectual Property

- Spending a disproportionate amount of time and money chasing technology

- Getting into verbal blog wars with people who can't be pleased/spammers

Section 3: More Detail on Intellectual Property Negatives

Step 1: First, What is Intellectual Property?

Following is a quick, very simplified overview of some of the types of "intellectual property" that might be involved in your business. You should always consult your attorney as part of your decision making process, so that your attorney can give you advice specific to your particular situation and needs. If your business involves any intellectual property, you should seek your attorney's advice for more advanced detail on the rules and scope of protection (and things to avoid,) so you can make the best intellectual property-related decisions and strategies.

- **Copyright -** Copyright is a legal concept that protects a <u>particular tangible expression of an IDEA</u> for a fairly long time (Example: If you are the author of a work you created after 1978, the copyright protection on that work ends 70 years following your death). What does it mean to protect "a particular expression of an idea" rather than the idea itself? If you write a love story, you own the copyright to that particular love story, but that doesn't prevent anyone else from writing their own love story. In other words, you own your particular expression of the idea of a love story, but you don't own every love story just because you wrote one love story. Copyrights cover things like music, writings, photographs, computer source code, videos. The government website detailing copyrights can be found at copyright.gov

- **Patent -** Patents protect a particular novel idea or process. Examples would be things like Cloning, Amazon's 1-Click (stores and retrieves your info on one click at check-out), genetically engineered plants, and specific non-obvious designs (such as an alligator pillow). Patents give you a monopoly over the idea itself for a limited period of time, after which time the idea is in the public domain. The exact duration of your monopoly (i.e., you patent protection) depends on the type of patent, but by way of example the time frame generally varies from 14 to 20 years. Timing is VERY important in the patent world, so if you think you have a patentable idea you need to seek advice from a licensed patent

attorney ASAP. The government website detailing patents can be found at
uspto.gov

- **Trademark -** A trademark basically protects the brand name/logo for your brand of goods. Common examples are Nike brand shoes, Coach brand handbags, Apple brand computers, Cheerios brand cereal, CocaCola brand soft drinks. A service mark is a category of trademark that basically is your brand of services, such as H & R Block brand accounting. A company can have multiple service marks and trademarks, such as General Motors having the trademarks GM, Chevrolet, Corvette, Suburban, etc.   A trademark can last forever, as long as you keep your renewals and filings up to date, continue to use the mark, and comply with the legal requirements. The government website detailing trademarks can be found at uspto.gov

- **Trade Secret -** Trade secrets are secrets such as formulas, processes and customer lists, that are vital to your business OR that might have value to other businesses. A trade secret will last forever as long as it stays…SECRET. A famous example of a trade secret is the Coca Cola syrup formula. The key then, is that you must keep trade secret information secret. If, for example, you post your secret on a social media site, such as Facebook, then it is no longer secret, and you lose your ability to enforce your trade secret rights. If apply for a patent then it is no longer secret. If you share the trade secret with someone who has not signed a confidentiality agreement, then it is no longer secret (even if the person orally swore to keep it secret, it's hard to prove). You can sue if someone steals a trade secret, but you will need to be able to show that you made a big effort to keep it secret, such as (a) requiring confidentiality agreements, (b) keeping the secret locked up, (c) limiting access to the secret to a need-to-know basis, and (d) prominently labeling all trade secret info as CONFIDENTIAL PROPRIETARY TRADE SECRET NFORMATION.

- **Trade Dress -** Have you ever noticed that all Starbucks look alike, and that it is eaqsy to recognize a Kentucky Fried Chicken or a Splenda packet of sweetener from a distance? Those visual cues are called trade dress. You can sue if another company tries to look the same as your company looks to lure in your customers. Sometimes the line between trademark and trade dress is very small, and you can have rights under both – in other words, you don't need to choose one or the other. Examples: Colors can be both trade dress and be trademarked, such as Mattel's Barbie doll brand pink or Tiffany's jewelry store box blue.

- **Right of Publicity –** There are laws that say that you can't make money off of a famous person's name or likeness without their consent. That law is why Wheaties & Nike need to pay athletes to use their names and likenesses, and that is why you shouldn't post photos of famous people without their consent.

- **Right of Privacy -** The flip side of the right of publicity is the right of privacy. There are laws that say you are not allowed to use a regular person's name or likeness without their consent. That is called a violation of an individual's right of privacy. That is why you see motion picture crews getting releases, etc., and that is why you shouldn't post photos of people on the web without their consent.

Step 2:   If You Post Something on the Web, What Happens?

1. You need to recognize that your "legal Rights" may not be the same as the practical ramifications of posting something on the web.

    a. Practical Ramifications of POSTING anything on the web:

        i. You lose exclusive control – digital is easy to transfer – see music industry outcome with Napster and how the whole music industry (spelled E-M-P-I-R-E) transformed. The music industry, using every tool at its power, including working together combining resources, ultimately won against Napster, but they lost the war anyway. The traditional music industry business model was crippled by the ease of digital copying, and since then record stores have gone bankrupt, and music industry now reworking and redefining itself with Apple iTunes pulling the digital copyright mess out of the fire. - Or, simply stated, it's one thing to own the copyrights to something, it's another thing to have the resources (manpower, time and money) to enforce your copyrights once the digital version of what you own is on the web.

ii.   Things seem to last forever on the web: Example: Websites are "cached" on Google, so even if you remove a webpage from your own server, your outdated website may still show up on Google for people to access (note: there is a process to remove Google cached websites, meaning you have to ask Google to remove the cached site; I don't know how compliant Google is, or the timing/complexity of the process, as I have never tried it myself)! For interesting definition and workings of cached on Google, see: http://www.googleguide.com/cached_pages.html

iii. Similarly, what you think is OK to write on a blog now can haunt you forever, hurt job opportunities, as it is much harder to remove items from the web than it is to post new items to the web! In other words, the web has a loooong memory.

Step 3:   Before you post anything on the web, look at the legal terms of the tools and hosts you will be using to do the posting.

1. First step before utilizing any service on the web, whether free or paid for, is to examine the legal terms, such as:

- What happens to control of the photos and content you send, post or create using their service? (The Intellectual Property Terms)
- Price (can they up the price on you once you have done a lot of work thinking the service waqs going to stay free?)
- Commitment to actual service & warranty (what are they actually going to do for you; what happens if site goes down, for example)
- Longevity (for how long will the service be available?)
- Can they change terms on you at the drop of a hat

2. Examples of Intellectual Property Terms:

   a. First let's look at **WordPress.com** blog intellectual property terms : http://en.wordpress.com/tos/ See for example section 2:

"By submitting Content to Automattic for inclusion on your Website, **you grant Automattic a world-wide, royalty-free, and non-exclusive license to reproduce, modify, adapt and publish the Content <u>solely for</u> <u>the purpose of displaying,</u> <u>distributing and promoting your blog</u>. If you delete Content, Automattic will use reasonable efforts to remove it from the Website, but you acknowledge that caching or references to the Content may not be made immediately unavailable."** **This might be the sort of language you would expect to see, whether for a blog or email or hosting your site.**

   b. Compare the above from Wordpress.com to the following Sections 6 and 7 of the **Salon.com** blog intellectual property terms located at: http://open.salon.com/support/terms:

Section 6 of Salon.com: "You understand and agree that any User Content you submit to Open Salon or post on the Site is intended to and generally will be made public, **and that once made public User Content cannot be made private again**. You consent to the public dissemination of all information you submit or post using the Service or the Site."

Section 7 of Salon.com: "By submitting or posting User Content using the Service or the Site, **you grant to Salon an irrevocable, perpetual, non-exclusive,**

13

transferable, fully paid, worldwide license to: (1) use, copy, publicly perform, publicly display, reformat, translate, excerpt (in whole or in part) and distribute the User Content in or through any medium now known or hereafter invented, for any purpose; (2) to prepare derivative works using the User Content, or to incorporate it into other works, for any purpose; and (3) to grant and authorize sublicenses of any or all of the foregoing rights. You may remove your User Content from the Site at any time. If you choose to remove your User Content, the User Content will no longer appear on the Site. However, you acknowledge that Salon may retain archived copies of your User Content, **and that Salon will retain the rights to the content granted by these TOS."**

      c.   In other words, you can see by comparing these two sites intellectual property terms that you really need to read these carefully, talk to your lawyer about the implications, and make your decisions wisely.

   3. Be watchful re anything you get in the "cloud" (paid for or not) or anything you get for free! Re the cloud – my personal opinion: don't rent when you can own!

CONCLUSION: Your "Legal Rights" are not always what you think/hope/assume, so you need to be aware and careful about what you post, where you post it, and don't post anything without considering both the practical and legal implications. You should always consult your attorney as part of your decision making process, so that your attorney can give you advice specific to your particular situation and needs. If your business involves any intellectual property, you should seek your attorney's advice for more advanced detail on the rules and scope of protection (and things to avoid,) so you can make the best intellectual property-related decisions and strategies.

Section 4:   Be aware you are making a Business Decision about each thing you post

After getting your lawyer's input, the final decision about whether to post, what to post and when to post, is you decision to make. Example:

•   Does what we learned in Section 3 mean we don't post on the web or use sites that have onerous terms?

- Not necessarily! For me, practically speaking, the moral of the story is that what you post (and therefore potentially lose exclusive control over) becomes a BUSINESS DECISION for you to make.

- Be AWARE! Don't let your eyes glaze over when you read the terms & conditions, and don't assume every website has the same terms and conditions.

- For me I generally only post things that, worst case scenario, I lose exclusive control over, but this needs to be a THOUGHTFUL decision after weighing the pros and cons of the reality of life.

- Look at terms and conditions of any agreement you "check to agree" to use the site

- Be aware of terms & conditions of online community journals/papers, some of whom try to get your advance consent to being able to reuse your submissions in any media (electronic, paper print, whatever) without paying you and without giving you credit as the author.

- Don't project what you want to be true (everyone is nice) onto terms and conditions that aren't "nice."

- Also, don't forget that the web is a GREAT research tool.

  - Whatever your field of interest, the web is a hugely valuable tool for researching how to do things in your business better.

  - You should look at how successful people in your field approach the web and social media and mobile.
    - What are they doing right that you can learn from?
    - What are they doing wrong that you can learn even more from?!

  - -And remember, just as you research others methods and customers via the web, they can research you!

Part 2 – Tailoring Your Web Presence to Your Customers

and Ensuring Your Website Finds and Serves Your Customers

by Knowing Your Customers

-So, with some caution as noted in Part 1 about what you put up and where, you need to get a primary presence online that your customers can find and that serves your customers the way they want to be served.

- You need something more than a blog, usually

- You need something more than a Facebook or MySpace page usually

- You need a REAL website!

- Your e-commerce, blog, general site, Facebook, Twitter, YouTube, etc. all should work together, and you need to incorporate innovations, like the mobile, tablet and e-reader worlds.

Section 5: Defining Your Website and Social Media Presence

The best way to design EXACTLY what you need, without wasting time or money, is to *know* what you need. Most of us have a basic guess, but if you take the following steps you will have a much deeper understanding of what your online presence needs to accomplish. Once you know what your online presence needs to accomplish, then you can efficiently design it.

Step 1: Start a "needs" outline by asking YOURSELF the following questions:

- How do you use the web?
- How do you use Facebook?
- How much time do you spend on Facebook each day?
- What other "social media" sites do you use, and how frequently?
  - Think about things like Twitter, YouTube, MySpace, Flickr, Lickedin, Tumblr, Yahoo

- Where do you shop online, and how frequently?
  - Amazon, iTunes, Craigslist, Ebay, Zappos
- Have you ever rated a purchase online? Where?
- Have you ever commented on a blog post or news article?
- What online hobby, professional, or interest communities do you belong to?
  - Examples might be ancestry.com, a website for a particular hobby, an investor website, a knitting website, a gardening website, etc.
- What email service do you use?
- What search engine do you use?
- What mobile devices do you use?
- How do you use those mobile devices?
- What apps do you use?
- Do you own a tablet?
- Do you own an e-Reader such as the Kindle or Nook?
- Do you own a Smart Phone?
- How much time do you spend on cell vs tablet vs computer?
- How does the way you use cell vs tablet vs computer differ?
- Have you ever used one of these:

Keeping in mind your answers for yourself to these questions, <u>if someone wanted to reach you or sell you something via the web, what would be the best way for them to find you AND engage you</u>?

Would they be able to find you on Facebook by searching for people with your favorite books, bands, travel destinations, or hobbies?

Key Point: If someone understands you and what you like, they will have an easier time reaching you with ads, especially via Facebook if you use Facebook. Facebook advertising lets you target your ads to, for example, something as specific as men over 50 who went to Cornell who list football and investing as interests, or a group as large as people who list their residence as California, or something even larger – all English speaking people. In fact, Facebook.com has a wealth of demographic information on each of its 500,000,000 users, and they sell access to it, via their ads, cheaply. SuperQuick™ Facebook outlines in detail how to use Facebook and create ads.

What other ways might someone trying to sell you a product/service find you?

Step 2: Defining who your customers might be and where to find them

The reality is, your answers to the above questions in Step 1 are just that: The answers for YOU. If you have a business, your customers might be like you and share your tastes and habits, but it is as likely that your customers are NOT precisely like you.

That means you need to:

- Ask your actual customers the same questions as in Step 1 above; AND

- Ask your prospective customers (the customers you would like to have) the same questions as in Step 1 above.

- When you add together your current customers and the customers you would like to have, you have started to define what in marketing is known as your "target demographic."

Why are these questions important:

If no one in your target demographic uses Facebook, then you should be cautious about spending too much effort there. However, if half your target demographic all belong to a particular gardening club website, then that gardening club website might be worth working out an advertising arrangement with.

The marketing terminology for understanding your customer base and prospective customer base is "knowing your target demographic."

- You can have more than one target demographic.

- The key is, your marketing campaign will probably be at least a bit different for each target demographic.

- *That means your web strategy depends quite a bit on your target demographics' respective tastes and habits – that is, their answer to the above questions.*

- A common error is to define your target demographic too narrowly. This results in a marketing and web strategy that is too undefined. Instead, try to define your target demographic as narrowly as possible by considering things such as:

  - age (such as people older than 55, or college age people, etc)
  - sex (men, women)
  - hobby (football enthusiasts, gardeners, sailors, scrapbooking, etc.)
  - other interests (motherhood, political party, investments, etc.)
  - Occupation (lawyers, artists, teachers, plumbers, etc.)
  - Geographic (living within a certain radius or city or state or country)

REMEMBER, you can have more than one demographic. A good marketing plan and web strategy targets each demographic separately.

Step 3: Asking Your Target Demographic Questions about THEM.

Now that you have a list of customers and a description of your target demographic, the next step is to ask your target demographic the following questions, that you already asked yourself:

- How do you use the web?
- How do you use Facebook?
- How much time do you spend on Facebook each day?
- What other "social media" sites do you use, and how frequently?
  - Think about things like Twitter, YouTube, MySpace, Flickr, Lickedin, Tumblr, Yahoo
- Where do you shop online, and how frequently?
  - Amazon, iTunes, Craigslist, Ebay, Zappos
- Have you ever rated a purchase online? Where?
- Have you ever commented on a blog post or news article?
- What online hobby, professional, or interest communities do you belong to?

o Examples might be ancestry.com, a website for a particular hobby, an investor website, a knitting website, a gardening website, etc.

- What email service do you use?
- What search engine do you use?
- What mobile devices do you use?
- How do you use those mobile devices?
- What apps do you use?
- Do you own a tablet?
- Do you own an e-Reader such as the Kindle or Nook?
- Do you own a Smart Phone?
- How much time do you spend on cell vs tablet vs computer?
- How does the way you use cell vs tablet vs computer differ?
- Have you ever used one of these:

- If someone wanted to reach you and share something via the web, what would be the best way for them to find you AND engage you?
- Would they be able to find you on Facebook by searching for people with your favorite books, bands, travel destinations, or hobbies?
- What other ways might someone trying to sell you a product/service find you?

In other words, you are conducting a "survey" of your target demographic. If your survey isn't too long or intrusive, surveys can be a great way of reconnecting with customers and of making relationships with new ones. Add the survey results to your "needs" outline started in Step 1 of this Section 5.

FREE ONLINE SURVEY creation and reporting tools: http://wufoo.com

FUN NOTE: To learn more about various demographics by zip code, there is a website that provides free access to demographics by zip code, in a fun way. See: You are where you live: http://www.claritas.com/MyBestSegments/Default.jsp

Step 4: Once you have incorporated the results of your survey into your 'needs' outline, then you are ready to design your web presence accordingly. This is the best way to ensure that your website actually serves your customers the way your customers wish to be served.

Once you understand how your target demographic uses digital media, go through each element of your needs outline created above, and ask yourself:

If I had a HUGE budget, what ideally:

- would I want my digital presence to accomplish (i.e., what are your goals for your site)?
- what should my website look like to accomplish these goals?
- what would my mobile presence look like to accomplish these goals?
- what would my social media presence look like to accomplish these goals?
- Does the tablet change anything for me?

Don't forget to scout out what your competition is doing – after all, they are trying to reach the same target demographic as you are!

- What is my competition doing right?
- What is my competition doing wrong?
- Can I learn my competition's customer lists from the web?
- Can I learn my competition's business plans from the web?
- Can I learn my competition's relationships from the web?

Now the final question, which this book will help you answer:

- What is the cheapest way I can do everything I want to do?

Part 3 – How to Get a Real Website on the Web- for free or nearly free

Now that you have determined who your target demographic is, how best to reach them on the web, and what your we presence should look like to best find and serve them, you need to implement your web presence. The first step to implementing your web presence is to have a place, a server, on the web that will host your website.

Section 6: Finding a host for your website

There are many free and paid-for sources of hosting on the web. Not every host offers the same capabilities – in other words, <u>your choice of host might limit the functionality and size of your site</u>.

If your web presence requirements are minimal, there are several easy ways to start for free, with free hosting and built-in predefined free templates, such as:

- http://yola.com or
- http://webs.com or
- http://weebly.com

However, finding a free host that offers a robust free hosting package can be more difficult. **The following is a FREE HOST that, as of the writing of this book, provides a very generous and robust free hosting package:** *http://www.000webhost.com* More specifically, as of the writing of this book, this free hosting site offers free hosting with 1500MB of free space and 100GB/month of data transfer, PHP 5 and MySQL, all free.

If you have access to uploading to a server that has PHP 5 and MySQL, such as the above free host *http://www.000webhost.com* or a paid for host such as http://hypermart.net, then you can use http://wordpress.org to create your website.

Section 7: Choosing the Software/Template to help you create your site

Now that you have a host for your website, you can actually build the design of your website.

- If you are using yola, webs, or weebly, you will find they offer pre-set templates, with pre-set functionality.
- If you have chosen a host that gives you more flexibility, such as free host *http://www.000webhost.com* or a paid for host such as http://hypermart.net AND if you know HTML or own web creation software such as Adobe DreamWeaver software, then you can design your site from scratch.
- Important Note: Even if you are using a host that provides flexibility to design your own site, there is no reason to design your website from scratch, because there are lovely, robust, user friendly templates out there, many of them available for free. In other words, I recommend you not try to reinvent the wheel, but rather that you start from a template that suits your needs. You can search Google for these free web templates.
- My recommendation/What I Use: Wordpress.org offers versatile free website templates that you can upload to your own server/host.

Wordpress.org templates are fairly easy to use. SuperQuick™ Wordpress shows you step-by-step, with illustrations, how to use Wordpress, from signing up for it through using advanced features.

Section 8: Learn Just a Bit of HTML

Just a little bit of knowledge of html will take you a LONG way, and will empower you to easily incorporate many useful elements into your website, such as e-Commerce, photo slide shows, survey forms, QRCodes, Facebook badges, Amazon affiliates products, Google Analytics (powerful free tools to help you track site usage), and much more.

How to learn HTML:

Because knowing HTML is so powerful and so useful, I recommend that you take a class in HTML or walk yourself through some of the free tutorials available online. Here are some excellent sources for learning html:

- Quackit.com - http://www.quackit.com/html/codes/

- Htmlcodetutorial.com – http://htmlcodetutorial.com/document

- w3schools.com – http://w3schools.com/html/default.asp

Common HTML question: I want to change the colors of the fonts or background of my site.   I was told I should choose a hexadecimal color. What are hexadecimal colors? How do you know where to find colors?

Answer: You can use a free online color picker to find the color you want. An excellent free color picker, also called a Hexadecimal color chart, can be found at:

http://quackit.com/html/html_color_codes.cfm

- You might hear that whatever you learn about HTML or coding will be out of date soon. That actually is not true. While technology and life keeps on changing, the logic structure of knowing coding and the detailed eye you need to have doesn't change. I have never regretted the time I spent learning HTML – it has opened up many doors for me, and saved me quite a bit of money in terms of not needing to hire people to maintain my site.

- If you like a site and wish to see the coding that makes it work, all you need to do is move your cursor to a background portion of the site you like, and then right click your mouse. When you do this, a drop down menu will appear by your cursor. From this dropdown menu by your cursor, choose "View Source".

Common Question: Should I Use Microsoft Word to write HTML?

Answer: In my opinion, no. While you can auto write a bit of html using Word, and then choose t h e "Save As" html command, this not the best way to do things-In my opinion, Microsoft Word is meant to be a word processor, not a web designer.

Why is it important to know HTML?

- So you can easily update things, maneuver, feel confident, not be held captive by a website developer
- So you can implement Google Analytics http://www.google.com/analytics
- So you can add FaceBook "badges" to your website, in order to integrate your Facebook presence with your main website presence
- So you can create effective Facebook pages for your business (see SuperQuick™ Facebook to learn how)
- So you can use Facebook ads and get super cheap demographic research
- So you can implement free survey forms:
    - http://www.wufoo.com and
    - http://www.emailmeform.com/

- So you can implement a free shopping cart, such as from http://www.fatfreecart.com/
- So you can take maximum advantage of stellar, easy to use, free expandable "blog" websites with free "gadgets," "widgets" and "plugins" like Wordpress.org and Blogger.com
- So you can use QR Codes on your site– free generator at http://quikqr.com/?p=qr-code-home
  - What is a QR Code?

  - QR codes are readable by camera phones/smart phones having the right app to red them. They are becoming increasingly popular. QR codes can store your phone number, email address, even have a linkto your webise or a secret message. You might wish to supply additional information or advertise using a QR code on packaging or in magazines, on signs, buses, business cards, or almost any other object you can think of.   Users with a camera phone having the right app/reader can scan the image of the QR code to display text, contact information, connect to a wireless network or open a web page in their phone browser.

  - Google's Android mobile operating system supports QR codes by natively including the barcode scanner (ZXing) on some models, and the browser supports URI redirection, which allows QR codes to send metadata to other existing applications on the device. Nokia's Symbian operating system also has a barcode scanner able to read QR codes, as do others, with the list evolving all the time. In the Apple iOS, a QR code reader is not natively included, but over 50 free apps are available with reader and metadata browser URI redirection ability.

- So you can use favicons as part of your branding (the little icon that shows up by your website address at the top of your internet browser window can be customized. See e.g. the little heart by the website address at http://Nicole.bz To learn how to create a favicon, go to http://www.favicon.cc

Section 9: Acquiring Adobe Photoshop will help you greatly

Adobe Photoshop is a software program that will greatly help you in the design, multitasking and maintenance of your site – in other words, the content you put on your site will be much more interesting if you invest some time and money into purchasing Adobe Photoshop. It is NOT free, but it is well worth the expenditure. You might wish to contact Adobe for a free trial so you can experiment with this software. Once you know how to use it, you will find it to be an incredibly valuable tool, not just for your website, but also for any marketing materials you might need to create. Following are some of the benefits of using Adobe Photoshop:

- Adobe Photoshop lets you easily resize, beautify, and meld your pictures. In fact, using Adobe Photoshop, you can change any image - whether colorwise, sizewise, or contentwise – to looking as you might wish it to be.

- Adobe Photoshop easily lets you overlay text onto your images.

- You can also use Adobe Photoshop to reduce the pixel resolution of your image, so it takes less time for your site to download for users. For web work, pixel resolution of 72 dpi (dots per inch) is usually fine. In contrast, for printing fine art greeting cards on paper, you would want at least 200 dpi. Adobe Photoshop lets you adjust those pixel dpi numbers quite easily.

- You can use Adobe Photoshop to create favicons (or you can go to http://www.favicon.cc)

Illustrated detail on how to size an image using Adobe *Photoshop:*

As shown below, in Adobe Photoshop, simply click the "Image" menu item, which then gives you the drop down menu shown below. From this drop-down menu, choose "Image Size"

Choosing "Image Size" from the drop down menu, as shown above, brings you to the pop-up menu shown below, where you can change the size of your image, and you can choose to work in pixels or inches.

 72 dpi is a fine resolution for the web. If you click the check box for "Constrain Proportions" then the relative dimensions of your original image will stay the same; if

that box is not clicked, then your image will be stretched to fit any new dimensions you choose. If I have to design to a particular size, such as 940x198 pixels for a Wordpress header, I either use an image that by itself lends itself to those dimensions or I use images with text to make up the difference in width; in other words, I would rather not stretch a single squarish image that far to be so much wider than tall unless I wanted a very abstract art look.

NOTE ON REDUCING RESOLUTION: In adjusting the pixel dpi numbers, always keep the original high resolution image unchanged, because it is easier to go from a high resolution to low resolution than vice versa. In other words, open the high resolution image in Photoshop, then save it as a new document under a new name, then reduce the image size only on the new document (leaving the original document untouched).

In short, Adobe Photoshop is the most valuable tool I use in working with website content and in creating my marketing materials.

Section 10: More optional things that you might wish to explore as time goes on

- In addition to learning HTML, a class in Java coding class might behelpful – Java does many things – forms, animations, useful with Apple products (as opposed to Flash)

- Consider learning Apple's environment, look into the Apple developer's SDK

- Adobe Dreamweaver – this is a fairly easy and semi pro way to create websites that you UPLOAD via FTP to a spot on the web that is your personal webspot on a server – i.e., your web host

- Adobe In Design (helpful with self-publishing, making eBooks, etc.)

- Possibly Adobe Flash (animations, Apple doesn't like it for now), Illustrator (vector graphics, harder than photoshop but lets you do smooth lines and interesting things with fonts).

- Wordpress.org worth exploring – see SuperQuick™ Wordpress for details.

- For shopping carts, if you wish to create your own from scratch, then it will be helpful for you to take a class in cgi/perl or php

- Again, make sure you learn at least basic html

- Look into Amazon's Kindle and Fire self-publishing platforms.

Section 11: Incorporating e-Commerce into your template

Odds are, you wish to have a shopping cart mechanism for your site. This section shows you how, and while the set-up may take some time, there are several free shopping cart mechanisms available via the web.

Before you start your own store online, remember you need to address the logistics:
- you need a way of collecting payment (step 1 below covers that),
- you need a way of tracking who buys what (this will vary depending on which shopping cart mechanism you choose in Step 2 below; the ecwid shopping cart mechanism of Wordpress.org does a nice job of this, for example)
- you need a way of keeping and tracking inventory,
- you need a way of fulfilling orders (called "fulfillment")(for a fee, places like Amazon can handle fulfillment for you, but these fees can be steep if you don't do it yourself.
- because your customers will need to see what they are buying, you will need 72 dpi photos and accurate descriptions of what you are selling to put on the web (Adobe Photoshop can be very helpful re the photos)
- you should talk to your lawyer and CPA to make sure you comply with the legal things, like sales taxes, warranties, export laws, can't sell to minors or violate privacy, etc.

Step 1: Sign up for payments processing

Signing a merchant agreement with American Express, Visa, Mastercard, etc. can be expensive, requiring you to pay hefty monthly amounts even if you don't sell much. Fortunately, there are lots of other alternatives to payment processing currently available, and these newer options essentially allow you to pay as you go, rather than commit up front.

Therefore, if you don't already have a merchant agreement with American Express, Visa, Mastercard, etc., then you might wish to consider the following in order to be able to process payments for most free shopping cart mechanisms:

- Sign up for http://paypal.com and/or
- Google Checkout.
- You might also wish to explore exciting new mobile phone payment options such as http://squareup.com as well as PayPal mobile: https://personal.paypal.com/us/cgi-bin/?cmd=_render-content&content_ID=marketing_us/mobile_payments

Step 2: Decide which Shopping Cart mechanism you wish to use for your site

The web offers many free shopping cart mechanisms, such as:

- http://www.fatfreecart.com/
FatFreeCart works with both Google Checkout and Paypal payment systems, and so can be quite handy. It gives you the code for you to cut and paste into your site. Some basic knowledge of html will be helpful in

using FatFreeCart.

- The Google Checkout Store Gadget (for use with Blogger, Google sites and others)

- The PayPal widget (for use with hosts such as Yola – see http://yola.com/tutorials/article/Tutorial-Creating-an-Online-Store-1285944434245/Adding-and-editing-content for step by step instructions

- The Wordpress free "ecwid" shopping cart widget – for an example of a ecwid shopping cart see http://artimagination.com (NOTE: SuperQuick™ Wordpress gives you detailed, illustrated step-by-step instructions on how to use the ecwid Wordpress shopping cart. Also: Remember not to confuse wordpress.org with wordpress.com – same folks run these sites, but .com is waaaaay scaled back!)

Step 3: Consider if other avenues of selling on the web are right for you

Make sure you explore selling via Amazon, Apple iStore, eBay, and other online sites

Section 12: How to FTP

If you design your own site or if you wish to upload something to your server, you might need to know how to FTP.

FTP is actually ridiculously easy in Windows Explorer. It's like browsing, copying and pasting from one directory on your computer to another. Here is how to FTP using Windows Explorer:

- Arrange/sign up for hosting, whether for free or with a paid host like Hypermart, and when you sign up for hosting, as part of that process your host will require you to choose a username and password.

- Once you've signed up for hosting, type in your server address in your Windows explorer browser – your host will give you this, it's not a mystery, usually something like ftp://snoopy.yourhostname.net

- After you type in your server address, automatically a login box appears, asking you for your username and password, which you know from when you signed up for hosting. The login box looks like what you see below:

- Once you are logged in, you will see whatever is on your server as a list as files, as shown below:

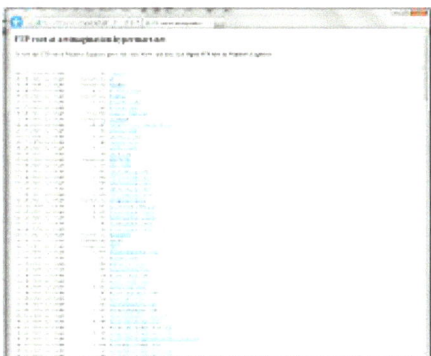

- To make life look more familiar, all you need to do is use Windows Explorer to "Open FTP Site in Windows Explorer." In new versions of IE, it means clicking <Alt> then <View> then <Open FTP site in Windows Explorer> as shown below:

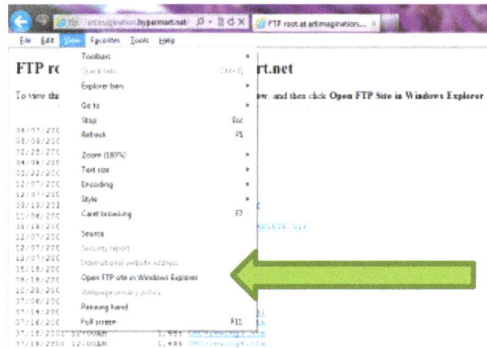

Doing the above step changes your view from a list of files to file folder icons, as you see below. Now it looks like what you always see when you browse through folders.

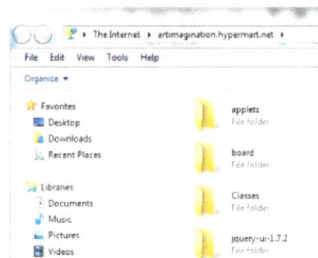

For older versions of IE: On the right menu bar of Windows Explorer, click the "Page" drop down menu, and from there click "Open FTP Site in Windows Explorer."

- From this point on, you can just browse and copy back and forth between your computer's hard drive to your host, seamlessly, just as you would between file folders on your hard drive. That's all there is to it!

Other info on FTP you should know for real life:

- There may be some security issues with FTP, because your login is not encrypted. Therefore some people prefer to use SFTP (see Wikipedia for more info on SFTP).

- Adobe DreamWeaver has ftp built in:

  http://www.columbia.edu/~abv5/Webpub/FTP.htm

- Overview of FTP at http://www.filetransferplanet.com/ftp-guides-resources/

- Can also see wiki page on FTP:

  http://en.wikipedia.org/wiki/File_Transfer_Protocol

- Oodles of video results on FTP, such as:

  http://video.search.yahoo.com/search/video?p=how+to+ftp+files

Section 13: What Else You Need to do

- Assemble Content for your site (again, Adobe Photoshop will help you make your images be the right size and look attractive.

- Reserve Domain Name (http://networksolutions.com is example of one of many who charge to reserve name)

- **TEST YOUR SITE BEFORE YOU PUBLICIZE IT!**

Testing your site is an excellent opportunity to get to know you target demographic better and to start building a customer database.

Section 14: How to Test Your Site

This is an opportunity to build community! Find someone who has never seen your site before and ask them:

- What do you see first? What do you notice first? Website visitors "bounce" from site to site quickly. Make sure the first thing they see will "buy" you more time.

- What do you think the main purpose of the site is?

- Did it take you a long time to figure it out?

- Did anything frustrate you about the site?

- Can you navigate it easily? Is it "user friendly?"

- Are the menu choices clear and accurate?

- Any dead links?

- Is it interesting?

- Is it attractive?

- Does anything about the site annoy you?

- How far did you have to scroll down or link to, in order to get to what you think is the main point of the site?

- Did you see anything that convinced you to purchase the product or service? What was it? Was it hard to find?

- Do you think it would be easy or hard to order something from this site?

- What image do the colors and images give you?

- Is the site too "busy"?

- Is the site too "basic?"

- Is the site easy to read? Many experts recommend using a simple, sans-serif font in a dark color with high contrast to a non-offensive, not too-busy simple background.

- Ask your user to try the site on his/her mobile phone and tablet. How did your site translate to mobile devices and to tablets?

    - Watch for things like iPhone vs Android. Did the Flash animation parts of your site still work?

- o Note that SuperQuick™ Wordpress shows how you can easily make a Wordpress.org based website work on mobile devices.
- Is your user familiar with QR codes, and did he/she experiment with any of them on your site?

MORE ON SITE DESIGN
A CHECKLIST FOR YOU TO CONSIDER IN DESIGNING YOUR SITE:

- o Is there an easy way to contact the business? Note that you can use a free survey form to also serve as a part of your contact us page. See e.g. http://www.wufoo.com or http://emailmeform.com
- o Is there an "about us" page? Is there a reason to share info re the owner or employees of the company? Consider sharing photos, since it is helpful in big internet world to associate a face with a business.
- o Is there a site map?
- o Check with your lawyer about any necessary Legalese, such as intellectual property notices, privacy notices, and, often of import to customers, WARRANTY info, return info, and service info.
- o Do your guests feel intrigued or engaged, do they want to stick around and explore more?   This is known as the "bounce rate" statistic, available for free using Google Analytics

- o Is the writing interesting? Is it in keeping with the brand image? Does it sound too corporate or too informal? Have you spell checked?
- o Have you copied anything from somebody else's site? Talk to your attorney to make sure you have the legal right to post the images, music, articles you use on your site.
- o Is your site too slow to appear? Is your site too bogged down with too much multimedia? Videos, podcasts, tutorials and photos are great, but they need to be done in a way that doesn't slow things down! Avoid too many bells and whistles.

o Have you used social media well? Did you explore/sign up for Youtube, Facebook, Twitter, LinkedIn and other social media sites thatmight help drive traffic to your business? Are there links to social media, like your Facebook page, so that you can build community? But watch for revealing your customer lists!

Part 4 – Driving Traffic and Search Engine Optimization

Once your main site is up and ready to go, the next step is driving traffic to it, and testing to see what works and what doesn't work in terms of spreading the word. The art of driving traffic to your site is an art more than a science. Part of what you do in terms of driving traffic to your site will depend on what sort of business you are in.

There are several ways to drive traffic to your site.

Traditional Print Media, Radio, etc: You could advertise in traditional print media to drive traffic to your site. For example, if you were a surf board company, you might advertise in a magazine with a QR Code linking to your site. If you sold hospital wear for nurses, you might try advertising in a hospital newsletter with a QR code. Advertising in some print media can be expensive, while others (like small organization newsletters) can be fairly inexpensive, even free if combined with interesting content. You could similarly advertise a catchy website name on radio, but again, that can be expensive. Most traditional forms of advertising have a cost to them, unlike the web, which can be done for very little (even free), if you know what you are doing.

Social Media: Social Media is essentially free, except for the time it takes to set it up and maintain it. In addition to your main site, you probably will need Social Media to most cost-effectively spread the word about your business and to drive traffic to your website. Social Media is still evolving, but current commonly used social media sites include Twitter, Facebook (more than 500 MILLION users), Blogger, Wordpress, Flickr, Linkedin, Tumblr, Bebo, Google Buzz, and MANY MORE, and new ones all the time. Social Media can also include the blog you keep on Wordpress.com or via your Wordpress.org custom website (see SuperQuick™ Wordpress to learn more about Wordpress.org custom sites).

Section 15: Nuts and Bolts of Social Media

Some basic steps to conquer social media:

1. Sign up and maintain a free blog – http://bloggercom or http://wordpress.com are among the many, or you can incorporate one into your custom wordpress.org site easily (see SuperQuick™ Wordpress to learn more about Wordpress.org custom sites).

2. Sign up and maintain a Facebook page (see SuperQuick™ Facebook to learn more about creating custom Facebook pages and advertising them).

3. Sign up and maintain a Twitter account

4. Consider signing up and maintaining other social media accounts, such as Linkedin, Flickr, etc (which social media accounts you sign up for depends on which social media sites your target demographic is likely to use).

5. Setting up each social media account is time consuming. Make sure you save in a safe and convenient place all the user names and passwords for all these social media accounts

6. Encourage interaction with your target demographic by offering something fun or of value (but don't give away the store), and make sure you promptly and professionally RESPOND to people who contact you.

7. Use the social media sites to seek people out, but I recommend you NOT give any of the social media sites permission to access your email contact list.

8. In using the social media sites, remember your competition might be watching – don't give away your valuable customer list or future plans! offer something of value (but don't give away the store).

9. You need to keep all your social media accounts fresh and current. Here is a CRITICAL shortcut, so that you don't need to log into each social media account separately! There are free sites out there that let you easily update all (or as many as you choose) of your social media sites with one single post! They are:
   a. http://ping.fm/ (free) or –
   b. http://www.hootsuite.com (partially free)

10. You need to keep having SOMETHING fresh to say – start taking photos, keeping notes, getting photo releases if people are in the photos.

11. Always link your social media sites to your main site (and vice versa – use things like FaceBook badges for example)

12. As we discussed in Part 1 of this book, you need to read the legal terms for EACH site. Remember not to assume the intellectual property ownership issues are fair, and don't post ANYTHING you want to keep control of. Make sure you work with your attorney on this.

Section 16: Google Analytics

Google Analytics is a wonderful FREE tool. It is available at:
http://www.google.com/analytics

- o Google Analytics let you track:
    - o how many new users come to your site (by day, month, year, whatever)
    - o how much time users spend on any particular page of your site,
    - o how many unique users you get (verses the same user reappearing),
    - o how the users of your site found your site (such as from search engines searches looking for your name or keywords (and Google Analytics will even tell you which search words the user input to find your site)(this type of traffic sometimes called "organic")
    - o Google Analytics will tell you how many people came from referring sites, such as your blog, and which referring sites (good way to see if an ad campaign is working, as well)

To sign up for Google Analytics, all you need is a Google Gmail account or Blogger account, etc to sign in.

Section 17: Search Engine Optimization (SEO)

While no one but the Google folks know their algorithm that determines where you fall in their search engine results (if you're not paying advertising fees), what we do know is that search engine optimization, also called "SEO," basically moves you up the search engine rankings.

To improve your SEO:

- Use lots of KEYWORDS in both your user-visible site content and in your site HTML meta tags: For a television repair site, keywords would be words like: tv, television, repair, service, {brand names}, flat screen, etc.

- Go to https://adwords.google.com/select/KeywordToolExternal and see how many people actually search for those keywords!

- Put keywords IN THE RIGHT PLACES. Not just meta tags (html code) but also use keywords in the title that appears when your page shows up, in your site headlines & subheadlines, in the first paragraphs of your website, even in articles – write with keywords in mind! The more you use those keywords, the stronger your SEO. It's that simple!

- INBOUND LINKS: This is where social media can really help you. Make sure you use links TO your main site from all your social media sites, including your blog, Twitter, Facebook pages, etc. Consider partnering (I link to you, you link to me) (but weigh if you really should be driving traffic AWAY from your site in the quid pro quo)

- Wordpress.org has several FREE SEO plugins, such as the one I use. REALLY REALLY EASY GOOD STUFF! SuperQuick™ Wordpress gives the details on this.

- Add your site to SEARCH LISTINGS – such as local yellow pages, and also, FOR FREE, you can add your site to: www.google.com/places which actually puts you on a map. (To start, when at that site, select "Add New Business"). ASIDE: This site lets you offer coupons!

- Paid advertising, such as pay-per-click Google Adwords at www.google.com/adwords For example, if you are willing to pay $20 a day, you will tell Google that for certain keywords you are willing to pay $2/click, and then Google will run your ad until you reach 10 visitors. You can then use Google Analytics to track results and see what changes you need to make to your adword campaign. Google ad planner at www.google.com/adplanner is a good resource for noodling out your adword campaigns, it shows you who goes to what sites, lets you find your demographic more easily.

- You can pay for ads on Facebook using the Create an Ad option on Facebook. Unlike Google, where you choose words for people to find you, on Facebook, you choose groups of people, like people who have the words "art collector" or "museum" in their profile. Facebook is unbelievably powerful way to test and find your demographic. SuperQuick™ Facebook gives the details on this.

- YouTube videos – like commercials, how tos, etc. can drive traffic to your site. If you get enough traffic, YouTube will even approach you about paying you if you are willing to place ads on your YouTube videos.

- Write articles for popular sites, with links to YOUR sites, but watch ownership of content issues – read the legal terms and conditions:
    - http://www.ezinearticles.com
    - http://www.goarticles.com
    - http://www.articledashboard.com
    - http://www.isnare.com
    - http://www.articlebiz.com

- Join affiliates programs, such as AMAZON – kindle, e-store, Associates and Affiliates programs, etc.

- Don't forget that QR Codes including on packaging and social media websites can drive traffic!

- Coupons, as through www.google.com/places

- Webinars, using things such as http://gotomeeting.com to host the meeting

- Events

- Contests – watch laws on this though!

- Provide good information (but not TOO much!)

- E-newsletters and e-Marketing – AVOID SPAM Words, and NOT too often or everyone will opt out

- Self Publishing – paperback, eBook, Kindle, Nook, iPhone, iPad, Fire
- PodCasts

MORE THINGS TO REMEMBER:

Online is a great way to build a customer list and enhance your business model, but if you are careless it is also a great way to give your customer list and business models away.

Remember also: You need to respond promptly and professionally to your customers, because of you don't have consistent and professional follow-through then your efforts are for naught.

M. Nicole van Dam, in addition to exploring Facebook, works in many media, such as oils, acrylics, water color, pastels, pen and ink, and silk. In each work, one can find a passionate celebration of nature's beauty and diversity, which is Nicole's primary inspiration.

Nicole, a California native born of Dutch immigrant parents, was educated on the East Coast and is now living by California's Central Coast with her much-loved husband, dogs and birds.

Nicole writes about her artistic endeavors, pets and vegetable garden at her news blog, Wishes.bz. Nicole's parents are a tremendously positive influence in her life, and she attributes much of her success and love of the arts to them.

As a California native born of Dutch immigrant parents and educated in the East, Nicole's work expresses strong West Coast, East Coast, and European influences, artistically blended with Nicole's unique Impressionist flair. Nicole's style and distinctive color palette gives each work a new feel which is joyously whimsical, and yet somehow also reminiscent of a time when life was less hectic.

Creating engaging works that inspire, enchant and cheer, Nicole has been forging her own unique niche in the art world, earning excellent reviews and various one-man shows. Nicole is also an internationally licensed artist/designer, as well as a published poet and author of adult and children's books. An example of a children's book that she wrote and illustrated is "Inca Dink, the Great Houndini" (please see www.IncaDink.com to learn more). She also authored "Tempo –The Rhythm and Rhyme of the Artist" – a fun and inspirational book for adults blending art, poetry and philosophy.

Dedication

This Book is Dedicated to my patient husband, Jay, and my two dogs and birds, who make me laugh.

Other Books by M. Nicole van Dam:

SuperQuick ™ Facebook

SuperQuick™ Wordpress

Tempo – The Rhythm and Rhyme of the Artist

M. Nicole van Dam, a Retrospective 2010

Inca Dink, The Great Houndini

The Background Story of Inca Dink, The Great Houndini

To learn more, please visit Nicole.bz

Gondolier of Venice ™

An example of a painting by M. Nicole van Dam.

About the Cover Art: *"Sailing™" is a painting by M. Nicole van Dam.*

All artwork used under license and © and ™ M. Nicole van Dam. Learn more about this art at Nicole.bz

www.ingramcontent.com/pod-product-compliance
Lightning Source LLC
Chambersburg PA
CBHW052055190326
41519CB00002BA/231